S0-BTT-887

The Undercover Yogi

Short Stories, Poems, & Affirmations

by
Lance Harrington

Copyright © 2013 by Lance Harrington
All Rights Reserved

This book is based on the true experiences of the author.
No part of this book may be reproduced, stored in a retrieval
system, or transmitted by any means, electronic, mechanical,
photocopy, recording, or otherwise, without
written permission from the author.

ISBN: 978-1466247208
Printed in the United States of America.

The print version of this book is printed on acid-free paper.

Seek the Divine
and you will realize that you are already
universally rich,

For the seeds of Spirit
are the investments of God.

—Lance Harrington

Dedicated to

My parents, George Harrington and Laura "Sparrow" Lapoint, my stepfather, Edd Lapoint, my sisters, Tawny Harrington and Moriah Harrington, my brother-in-law, Carlos Reynosa, and my nephews, Kilo Reynosa and Mecino Reynosa.

Win

Thai Buddhist Master.

Helen

A truly wonderful person.

Thank you to Jessica Vineyard of Red Letter Editing (www.redletterediting.com) for editing this work and to Jeff Altemus of Align Visual Arts & Communication (www.alignarts.com) for the book design.

With love, respect, and appreciation.

Contents

Acknowledgments xii

Introduction 1

Our Journey 4

A Simple Prayer Intention 5

The Affirmations

An Affirmation.. 8

Giving Fully 9

Love in All Hearts 9

Aligning Our Holy Temple................................10

The Angelic Light... 11

The Unfolding Love 12

The Divine Love..12

The Universal Love 13

The Highest Love...13

The Presence of the Spirit 14

Awe and Wonder..15

The Spirit of Joy 15

Our Planet Glowing 16

Unity for All People 17

Spiritual Satisfaction 18

The Beauty...18

Full Gratitude 19

Illuminated 20

The Poems

The Undercover Yogi 22

Dear Buddha, Jesus, Quan Yin,
All Beings of Pure Light.................................... 23

Yin Yang.. 24

The Universe.. 25

Finding My Heart.. 26

The Zen Sets.. 28

Meditative Mind and Spirit Strength.................. 29

Eternal Love.. 30

Where I Find God.. 31

A Walking Miracle.. 32

Heaven's Daily Food.. 33

Star Messages.. 34

Meditation Mind.. 35

The Rain... 36

When We Know.. 37

Forever Loyal to My Heart................................ 38

Action Reaction... 40

Truth.. 40

The Courage.. 41

Remembering Our Intuition.............................. 42

Heart Open... 43

Love, Newly and Eternally Experienced............. 44

My Love Reaches the Heavens.......................... 45

Meditation.. 46

A Flower's Essence.. 47

Tree of Life... 47

Life.. 48

Relationships.. 49

Reflection..50

Sun Cloud 51

Kiss of Life...52

Depth of the Soul...52

Soul Strength...53

Divine Parents 53

Stimulating Love 54

Essence of the Soul...55

The Battle 56

Opening the Heart..57

Universal Law...57

For Your Heart..58

Together 59

Love Medicine 60

Intuitive Spirit 60

True Happiness...61

Divine Within 61

Fairy Dust...62

Walking Faith 62

Self-Love and World Love 63

Dreams 64

Learning Love Is Our Daily Practice..........................65

Remember 66

The Light Comes Through...67

Star Teachers 68

In the Breath of a Moment 69

Giving Thanks to God's Omnipresence
    and Beauty 69

A Little Poem 70

Feeling Real Love Is Our Greatest Experience 71

Love 72

Soul Preparation.. 73

Enjoying Life 74

Love Is All There Is 75

Word of the Heart... 75

Patience, a Treat of God.. 76

Hearing the Angels Whisper 77

My Meditation Altar 78

God's Flowering Essence 79

Our Freedom 80

When Love Pours In 81

This Is Our Home 82

Love Is My Religion 83

Love Comes In 84

Eternity... 85

Everything Everywhere.. 86

The Planet Teachers.. 87

Knowing 88

Perspective.. 89

Seeing Eternity 90

For All Beings 91

Gentle with Yourselves Always.................................. 91

Universe Creator... 92

Water of Beauty 93

Meditate.. 94

Meditate.. 95

A Spiritual Age on the Planet 96

Nature Sounds 97

Expressions of Love and Beauty 98

A Simple Poem: The Love for Our Earth,
   Sun, and Moon 99

The Light within Us 101

Earthly Mother 102

Love and Light 103

Happy Birth Day 104

Honoring the Women on Mother's Day
   or Any Day 105

Natural Giving on Easter or on Any Day 106

The Deities Are for All 107

A Yogi's Heart and the Guru Within 108

The Warrior Soul Joining Together
   with the Spirit Mind: A Metaphor 110

The Love Poems

Reminder 112

For Love I Bow 112

Life is My Greatest Relationship 113

Gifts of Life 114

To Love 114

Soul Mate 115

Love Is Falling from the Sky 117

Divine Love 118

Divine Blue Skies 119

Eternal Light 120

Springs of Joy 122

Divine Beloved...124

Love Uniting 124

Angelic Love 125

Merkaba Galactivation 126

Heavenly Play 127

Open Doors in the Universe 128

My Divine Lady 129

To Love I Bow 130

Love in the Setting Sun 131

Surviving Love 132

Short Stories

Reincarnated to Remember Birth, Death,
    and Eternity...134

Awakened to Divine Sleeplessness 135

A Story of Our Guru Mind and Our Other Mind:
    Coming Together to Be One,
    in Simple Meditation...................................... 141

A True Story of a Buddhist Master and
    My First Meditations 143

Sensing the Spirit: The 80-Year-Old
    Buddhist Virgin 144

The Glowing Buddhist in the Picture...................146

The Day of Awakening..147

The Devoted Buddhist 149

An Amazing Woman and Her Divine Gift 151

The Devoted Woman and Her Gift............................153

The Body and the Universe's Voice........................154

Intuitive Voice..155

Divine Intention 155

Expressions of the Heart......................................156

Benefits of Meditation 157

Divine Love: Simple Tools for Meditation...................158

The True Value Giver 160

The Golden Chain....................................... 161

I Live for Divine Awakening for a Living 162

Love to All People, for a Spiritual Age Is Near............163

You are the one... 164

Always Count Your Blessings

Through the Universe and Back...................166

We Are the Chosen Ones 167

Within You...168

Acknowledgments

Thank you to my family; you are the sunshine on my angels' wings. Thank you for your warm, pure, and bright golden love. I am deeply grateful for you. Thank you so much for loving me and teaching me to always see the beauty in all of life. Thank you to all my friends for always being there with your hearts wide open.

To Master Win for your love and care; your beautiful heart reflection and spiritual discipline lit more flames of love within me, inspiring me and sprouting little seeds that were already within me to be a healthier, happier, and more compassionate loving being for all beings. You openly lived and shared the benefits of having a meaningful and highly fulfilling spiritual practice and you helped give me a taste of that joy.

Helen, thank you so much, you truly saved my life and inspired me to live, always to stay positive and remain disciplined every day to my meditation practice.

Introduction

The purpose of this book is to promote meditation and to inspire the genius within everyone. Through long hours of meditation, writing poetry, speaking positive affirmations, and doing an EEG test, I found all the proof I needed to share with you the idea that meditation can benefit people of all ages. When I finally opened up like a lotus flower to experience the nectar of the inner wisdom in meditation, I felt the extreme benefits. I then realized that many people don't know about it or know how to do it. So this gave me a strong, passionate mission to tell whoever I can about meditation.

In my 20s after many years of hardships and pain, I had an amazing healing experience and learned firsthand the benefits of meditation, which continues to strengthen my heart and mind. I believe that all material in this book was channeled through Spirit, so in a way I feel I can take only so much credit for sharing these writings. I wrote this book to show my gratitude to all the people who share hope, love, and kindness with humanity. May all people help one another to realize that we are divine beings and that we all share the right to live our lives until our natural deaths. May each person have enough food, clean water, and shelter, regardless of the political or religious circumstances arising from the minds of the people or in the minds of the people of our governments. I believe this world can and will work together to accomplish a unity so that everyone's basic needs can be met.

As you peruse these pages, remember one thing. God is everywhere, all the time, in everything. These poems and stories may carry some wisdom for you, but without your own inward introspection, these words only spread so much essence of self-love and God realization. I hope this book brings you more self-realization, gives you tools to expand your emotional and spiritual maturity, and brings you a greater awareness to carry with you throughout your entire life. May you find what you are looking for.

Through the affirmations, poems, and short stories in each of these pages, know that they are spiritually induced by the spirit of truth and love. May you enjoy the glorious mysteries and wonderments of love and the beautiful awe of where it all comes from.

Let us see the beauty and the gifts in each of our lives and may we be grateful to all those who came before us as well as those yet to come. What joy it will bring to all who assist in this beautiful cause to balance poverty and riches, and what joy it will bring to all the poor whose cries reach up to the heavens daily!

I had an opportunity to be tested by a professional who used an electroencephalogram to see what the brain really does when it is in meditation. The EEG measured and recorded the electrical activity of my brain. Special sensors (electrodes) were attached to my head and hooked by wires to a computer. The computer recorded frequency levels of my brain and showed them on a screen. The EEG showed that there were extreme differences between when my eyes were closed and not meditating and when I was meditating. The machine proved that meditation is, in fact, an extremely powerful way to get the brain to be in a better state for healing to occur, allowing it to normalize.

During meditation my brain was in a different state of being. It peaked high in alpha waves! I learned that alpha waves only happen when we are between dreaming and being awake. This is some great scientific data we were so grateful to find, and what a beautiful synchronicity it was that my friend worked for a doctor who had this machine at her work. This is a beautiful confirmation for us all to know clearly that meditation is a very effective practice and great for an overall healing of the mind, body, and spirit.

A daily dose of meditation gives us a chance to really tap into our hearts so the practical mind and the heart can work together. We are always receiving information from the universe before, during, and after we meditate.

I hope my poetry and affirmations are helpful for inspiring the yogi or yogini within you. The word *yogi* in Sanskrit means one who practices yoga. *Yogini* simply refers to the feminine version. Yoga is a commonly known generic term for physical, mental, and spiritual disciplines that originated in ancient India. There are many different types of yoga and ways to go deeper within to connect with our higher self. There are many yogis who meditate and aspire to live in a more self-realized awareness as compassionate, aware, loving beings on Earth. We may not wear Buddhist robes, but I assure you that there are many of us— undercover yogis—in the world doing great works. Many people have no idea that we are here, but what a blessing that we are!

Our Journey

One of the biggest things to know as a human being,
is to realize we are loved so much more than it
may seem sometimes,
and to know the universe loves us more than we can imagine.

Feeling, remembering,
and comprehending the universe's love,
is why we are here.

A Simple Prayer Intention

Spirit, may we always sense your presence and spread your light.

May we always feel your love in whatever mortal struggles we experience.

Let us always spread your love from the spirit of truth to all,

the love we feel and crave so dearly within our own hearts and minds.

May we always seek and see the truth,

always seeing your beauty in all things.

Let us always remember your light shines even in the bowels of the sleeping tortoise.

And let us be still and look forward to the days when we will see peace in the hearts of all people throughout our whole world as we come closer to a spiritual age.

Thank you, angels, for your patience with all human beings.

Thank you, angels, for always being there, waiting for us to recognize the spirit of truth within us, which you work hard to instill so unconditionally in the minds of all mortals, slowly evolving us closer to the universal loving unity for all beings,

bringing us all closer to the realizations of our individual divine purpose,

to a life of learning, and remembering to love more abundantly as we evolve closer and closer to a more spiritual life on our own journey into eternity.

The Affirmations

Now I gift you with the poetry, prose, and positive affirmations I wrote after long meditations.

Reading and especially writing out positive affirmations for ourselves is such an amazing spiritual tool for us, to affirm and call in a more positive frequency to our whole being. Practicing manifesting the highest attainable and most fulfilling life for ourselves with this tool, we become creators in our own lives and observe our beautiful affirmations come true in our day to day lives.

An Affirmation

I want to see the best happen for all people,
mind and body, spirit and spirit.
I want to see the bountiful universe
be realized within all our minds,
so we may sit in truth,
beauty, and understanding
of our divine universe
and spread the light back to whence it came!

Giving Fully

I want to see myself be conscious in all ways,
I want to be present with everything in front of me,
I want to feel healing in the essence of the presence,
I want to see every part of myself that can be tuned up,
so that I may look at it and it starts to be cleared,
so that I may give fully of myself,
to all my brothers and sisters.

Love in All Hearts

I want to see the best for all people in life,
I want to see what is the best of others' highest good,
I want to see love full in the hearts
of all the people of the Earth,
making us super human loving beings!

Aligning Our Holy Temple

I want to see love all around for all beings,
I want to see us all be expanded in consciousness,
I want to know truth when it enters my holy temple,
I want to feel peace with all who stand forth,
I want to see the high orders of light
bring us more to alignment,
with ourselves and the Earth.

Let us be ready.
We are ready!

The Angelic Light

I want to see love blossom into my soul so abundantly
that I could not even remember
what it was like to have never experienced it.
I want to see the light of the universe
flow through each soul and cover the whole planet,
where we all feel and see its glow of angelic light.

The Unfolding Love

I want to see the unfolding of the universe's love,
be realized by each evolving soul,
the realization that we are truly loved and adored
by our guides and creators.
I want to see the love from this realization
help all mankind to have comfort in the knowing
that we are being watched over and cared for
by the energies
that come with pure light.

The Divine Love

I want to see my strength,
my wisdom,
my power,
my body,
my spirit,
and the universe
work through me
to get done what is divinely wanting to be done
by my internal essence of divine love.
I send a blessing to the universe!

The Universal Love

I want to see the love in everyone's hearts be full and joyful,
so that we all can move on,
and be still,
in the knowing,
that we are truly, universally loved.

The Highest Love

I want to see my heart open so much
that the universal glow of light
can shine through me
with nothing from myself getting in the way.
I want to see my purpose be experienced
and to unfold
in the highest love and light.

The Presence of the Spirit

I want to see the love inside me be strong,
and powerful enough for my angels
to eliminate any negativity and transform it
into positivity in my life,
in all ways.

May anyone who is in my presence,
and in the presence of the spirit within me,
feel the same.

From my higher wisdom.

Awe and Wonder

I want to see the love that we all have inside us
blossom abundantly
into something we all look at in awe and wonder,
to remember it was there all along.

The Spirit of Joy

I want to see a beautiful soul mate in my life,
to love and adore,
to spread more the magic gift of love,
to all people!

Through the energies that come
from the spirit of joy.

Our Planet Glowing

I want to see the light shine on all of the planet.
I want to see the love of the universe
dissipate the shadows in mortal minds.
So in this, when the invisible veil is lifted,
we can connect straight to our angels and guides even more.
So we can treat the planet and ourselves
in the vision that the creators and life carriers had
and shared a long, but also a very short, time ago.
That love is with us still,
it is here with us.
I send love to our ancestors,
fairies, angels, life helpers,
and all spirits of pure golden light.

Unity for All People

I want to see the world be uplifted in light all over the planet,
with families in joy and love.
Filled with joy, with all their simple needs met.
I want to see the planet work together for one common goal,
to make it a priority,
to feed,
provide shelter,
and have clean water,
for all the world's people.

Spiritual Satisfaction

I want to see and be in full vibrational frequency
with the angels
and my higher wisdom within my body.
I want to see this fill my mind, body, and my spirit
with joy,
love,
and spiritual satisfaction
with the divine.

The Beauty

I want to see my life unfold and blossom
like a thousand flowers being observed,
with little giggling children dancing and playing,
observing beauty in a mystical land.

Full Gratitude

I want to see love overcome all things in mind and body,
I want to see the spirit fill the mind and body
in joy, truth, and beauty.
I want to see this raise the frequency,
So that one day the whole planet is on a living life,
in a full gratitude and love for all life vibration.

Illuminated

I want to see the love inside my being vibrating so strongly,
illuminating my whole being.
I want to learn all I need to learn,
to be a leader and a teacher of love.
I want to see happen
what is the highest and best for all people.

The Poems

The Undercover Yogi

Love and peace to my heart.
I remain filled with life's breath another moment,
walking in peace, with a glow of golden light.
I glide forward in life, persistent to strengthen myself,
to walk more calmly on this Earth.
Green trees whisper to my ears,
and ask my eyes to see them
and to hear their words.
To see them
and to feel them sincerely.

Here we all drink the waters of gratitude
for all of life.
We do our best, and that's all we can do
to attain perennial peace with ourselves
and the Earth.

Dear Buddha, Jesus, Quan Yin, All Beings of Pure Light

Your writings have spread your hearts to the wind,
landing down on our hearts.
You put your feet on the Earth.
We can feel you,
your love, your touch,
so very much.

Your essence and care bring life and magic to the air.

Your soul is like a sail that drifts us closer to eternity.

Yin Yang

Break free from the bondage of desire.
Take heed and be the golden compass that people look upon.
Do not be caught by feelings of unworth,
dragged behind a horse,
desperately trying to hold on.
Use your wit and might of an evolved animal,
to set in stone the strength of armor,
to have super powers of love,
to yield to the forces that be.

The Universe

Strengthen the divine inside you,
and love will undoubtedly overflow into the world.

Finding My Heart

I searched my whole life for a Guru,
to ask a simple question.

I asked the Guru, "How should I live my life?"

He said, "Live righteously."

I asked, "How do I do that?"

He said, "Always follow your heart."

I asked, "How do I follow my heart if I don't know where it is?
What is the best way to find it?"

He said, "In simple meditation."

I asked, "When I sit in meditation what should I feel or say?"

He said, "Feel the love for yourself, your family and then all beings.
Say to yourself,
'I am here to sit with myself.
I am here to sit with my Higher-Self,'
and sincerely mean it."

I asked, "Then what do I do?"

He said, "Focus on your breath and hear the sounds of quiet.
When thoughts come in, don't pay attention to them;
just keep focusing on your breath.

"Know that what you are doing is helping yourself to
connect with your heart.
Know that every time you meditate you're receiving little bits of
information you will need on your journey."

I asked, "Is that all?"

He said, "Feel comforted by your angels who are by your side.
Imagine them there . . . know that they are there,
because they truly are."

He said, "You will feel better and better through your
meditation practice
and one day you will be a leader and a teacher."

I said, "Thank you, teacher, for all that you do."

He said, "Thank you teacher, for all that you do."

I wrote this after my first meditations with a Thai Buddhist Master at sunset.

The Zen Sets

We watch forever in one moment.
The rays and waves of the sun,
put us in dream state,
bliss.
I think of all the sunsets that have ever been,
and all those yet to come.
I think of all the people who have seen them,
and still see them.
I think of all the people all around the world,
at one time,
watching the same sunset.
The sun represents, to me,
the forever end to a forever beginning,
the yin yang, the song never sang.
The moment, then,
is one that we will never see again,
for the sun goes down,
and will rise somewhere else,
and so might we.
Nor will we see the sunsets always the same.
Our eyes constantly changing,
new perception.
All we have is this moment,
so we must search for joy.

Meditative Mind and Spirit Strength

My mind well rested in meditation,
just enough spirit walking to need me little sleep.
I awake hearing birds of praise,
singing hellos to the morning sun
bursting with light over the mountain rocks.
The moment's meditations bring me a thousand years of peace.
Oh, how I remember meditating ceaselessly in a past life.
Bring me Earth to nurture my bones,
bring me wind to hear your message,
bring me love across the sun,
bring that heart's fire from a soul mate burning with ecstasy,
to join together with my eternal fire for the divine.
Bring me rainwater to wipe my body's growing pains away.
Bring awareness to thyself,
to know it is in thyself all along.
For I will give back to you always, universe,
what you've always given me.

Eternal Love

My heart gives, open, transmuting all unknown into pure faith.

Eyes wide open, glistening, looking into the womb of the sun.

This new mystery holds only the positive attributes and acknowledgment of an eternal blessing unfolding.

Excitement, joy, clarity, strength, courage, gratitude, optimism, and more love. I know the Mother and Father are holding our hearts.

I sit, sipping the wind and the candy blue sky.

Peace falls from the ashes of our love; love falls from the clouds of our heart.

Let us drink. Let us toast to eternal love.

I was inspired and did my first vipassana meditation at my home—seven to ten hours of meditation per day for one whole month. I wrote this the following in the fourth hour of the first day of my own version of vipassana.

Where I Find God

I sat in meditation,
and I was asked a simple question.
The voice asked, "Who are you?"
It then asked, "Are you your voice?"
I thought to myself . . . *No.*
It asked, "Are you your body?"
I thought to myself . . . *Well, kind of.*
It asked, "Are you your mind or your imagination?"
I thought to myself . . . *A little bit, maybe.*
I then thought to myself . . . *What am I?*
The deeper and deeper I went, the more I realized that
the deeper I dug into myself,
the more I am I find.
Within this there are no walls,
only truth.
I then thought to myself . . .
Awe,
this is where I drink tea with God,
in quiet meditation.

A Walking Miracle

The Earth is a happier place
with your loving heart presence here.

The city captures your light
and filters the air with it.

Your positive heart gives meaning
to a concrete jungle.

Your beauty
sends angelic butterflies out
Whereever you are.

The gift of spirit
whispers in our ears

To once again tell us
That we are always home.

Inspired from a week long fast.

Heaven's Daily Food

My stomach was empty, but my spirit is still free.

My heart was hurt, but I am still me.

My emotions were bound, but my heart still pounds.

I thought my thoughts were winning, but the Earth keeps spinning.

A lightning bolt of God's love strikes this mind,

Heaven and Earth is what I find.

The destiny of service springs to the surface,

Illuminating my body temple with all the nutrients it needs. God grants me all the Earth seeds tenfold, to keep my body alive and growing old.

My hands hold a prayer position, my intuition wide open to listen.

Gaining momentum closer and closer to home, a paradise they call the golden throne.
Reach for the sky, Earth children.

Reach for the sky!

The tree of life still exists.

Star Messages

When we look upon a star,
that's when we find out who we are,
the light shines, binds and blinds us,
in the love that we seek.
A peeking spark flies,
from the flickering star's eyes,
to tell us its ancient story.
We observe it in its full glory.
Even light years away,
other beings and stars pray,
sending their love from so far away,
reaching us where we stay.
Through their light, we unite,
observing their ancient story,
together.
Remembering we are all stardust,
always and forever.
Through the Earth and the sounds and the birds all around,
we hear the star's message
that we all share this sacred ground.
So from these loving stars we find,
that through the heart,
and a calm mind,
we find,
they planted a seed
for each human that they read.
A seed that will grow,
to remember and one day know,
that we are all divine stardust
and we all deserve to know
and grow.

Meditation Mind

When the mind is still and calm,
truth enters the ears clearly,
like music echoing through a tunnel.

The Rain

The rain so gentle in its strength,
a time the dirt is alive like us.
The clouds say we cry for you,
the plants say we grow for you.
A thousand years of peace,
a breath of life,
the rain whispers its moisture to my lungs.
A billion reminders of my thirst for truth.

When We Know

When we know ourselves first,
then we might have something to teach.
When we learn to know ourselves,
we can better understand humanity.
When we know our own humanness,
then we can have more compassion for others.

Inspired by stories of Jesus and Hafez, a Persian mystic poet.

Forever Loyal to My Heart

O, Eternal Mother, Eternal Father, I have given myself away
to those I did or did not seek.

I have met someone else
for thee and thine own love have pushed me away.

With open arms
I have left someone else,
for they too
asked me to stay.

I have also left myself,
for I chose to stay with them.

O, Eternal Mother, Eternal Father, I give to you.
I am here to lift them.
I gave to myself, for I am the unbroken one.
My heart is made of pure gold.

What does this day bring?
A cloud, or a whisper?

How does the sun beam?
Is it a love, will it gift her?

Ocean,
why does the Earth cry?
Will the moon try and lift her?

How will the birds sing
to every human being?

Will the sky give to you, like the hearts of so many
wise ancestors, and masters?

Brave spirits
lift up your heads
for God's light shines on you.
Lift up all your skulls,
for God has given life to so many before us.

Can you see now?
Your humble hearts,
beating, and glowing?

Filled with grace and love,
in remembrance
of the eternal blessing.

God has been giving you this life;
please don't forget again.

Earth, Wind,
Fire, Water Spirits.
I live for good.
My love is for God,
my wine glass is full and overflowing.

For he and she
have given me day.

The Divine has given me breath.

Action Reaction

Positive things you set forth for yourself
will unfold in front of you
like sweet loving gifts down the road.

Truth

When awareness becomes our law,
then we will no longer need laws,
and that will be our order.

The Courage

I strive for perfection,
I wish to fly,
filled with inspiration,
a tear to my eye.

Thoughts of freedom,
tingle my feet,
sounds from the drum,
I can hear its heartbeat.

Thoughts of love,
thoughts of peace,
thoughts of people walking free.

Thoughts of the land,
thoughts of the ocean,
thoughts of our lives in motion.

Thoughts from the stream,
I awake out of a dream,
and walk into the dream.

Remembering Our Intuition

Remember we are here learning to remember
how to navigate intuitively within time and space,
in all the different dimensions on this planet.
We look to our inner selves and our guides for strength.
And with people,
if they are listening to their higher wisdom,
we can share some truth with their angels and guides.
But because people's minds are so easily swayed
into the mind of worry,
listening and praying with our guides
will help us in some ways much more.

The meditative mind of us all
will lift us and the Earth back up,
connecting our awareness back to her
so she can nurture us again
with mutual respect and love.

To our mother and father,
our inner selves, the Earth, the universe,
and the light helpers.

Heart Open

Keep your heart open at all cost,
for your open heart is not just for you,
your open heart is for our whole world.

Your open heart shines light on the path for others
and helps guide them home.

For ourselves and the people,
we open our hearts for the world.

Love, Newly and Eternally Experienced

Love sprinkles to a new tide, I happen to receive
all the infinity inside.

My body temple pure in beauty, every moment in eternity is newly
seen, experienced, and dreamed.

We are connected to the sun, the trees, and the stars.

The universe shines its glow of light down for us to feel.

Let us sit and watch while we emit more signs
of God's eternity.

My Love Reaches the Heavens

My love reaches the heavens, my mind full of sevens.
The spiritual number, my intuitive hunger. For eternity,
I am divine energy, beautifying as angels move and
groove through me,
expanding my cells with light and the memories of star dust.
Galactivated like no other, brother, giver, soul inspired lover.
In the cosmos I know God flows through me. So you see?

I love you, and my love reaches the heavens.

Meditation

Feeling the calmness of your breath.
The quietness and sound of your heartbeat.
The feelings of not knowing,
The feelings of knowing that there is a connection to
the higher self.

A Flower's Essence

If we cannot hear the flower's voice,
then we shall sit longer in our daily meditation,
'til eventually one day we can hear the flower say it's okay
to pick of its beauty.

Tree of Life

The trees stand strong,
while the petals fall slowly and sit firm on the ground.

Be firm with your faith and love,
have patience,
and let your worries and pains fall to the ground.

Within this peace
we hear a voice in the wind,
we hear the songs of freedom.

Life

Starting something when you don't know how it will turn out,
finding materials that you will use,
imagining what can be made,
and making it,
and it changing as you go.

Life is art.

Relationships

Learn to be sensitive to others in relationships,
and you become a master of yourself.

Reflection

My eyes sprinkle with tears for all the years of fears.
My eyes shedding,
heading toward something new,
a true feeling of bliss that I missed.

Just by a flick of a wrist,
I stand waiting to unfold,
as a hold, a mold, ready to unfold.

A taste of a memory,
harmony,
I dreamed of this.

A dream seems so real,
flying,
soaring,
I awake to see morning.

Sun Cloud

Fill your cup with a cloud of laughter,
So you may drink it up and find joy in your life
with all the things that rain upon you.
We are a cloud, we are the sun,
And we all come from all the elements.
Without the clouds and without the sun we would not be,
We would not grow.
We are sharing our life with everything we see,
All the elements all around us.
We are everything and everything is us.
We all come from one big beautiful creation.

Kiss of Life

Let the kiss of life bring laughter to all those seeking the divine.
Universal Spirit, bring seraphic vision to our eyes to see
God's beauty in all things always.
Let the hands of all Earth beings be gentle and soft,
To touch each other's hearts with love and grace.

Depth of the Soul

Treat every day like it is your last.
Tell the people you love
that you love them.
Maybe even those you don't,
because there is a spark of God in everyone.
This sends a good vibration to you,
the universe,
and our world.

Soul Strength

Even if we view our lives as mundane,
as evolving creature souls,
we are still here expanding our hearts and minds.
So even in this
we are here expanding our soul.

Divine Parents

Understanding: the mother spirits
are involved as much as the father spirits.
The ones we speak and pray to.
It feels natural from our earthly home
and our human experience,
that there are feminine and masculine spirit energies
working together.
When it is understood that there are both kinds of Divine love
being shone down upon us
from our vast universe,
we can send our intentions to the great spirits,
feeling more at ease.

Stimulating Love

Love is the best stimulation;
remember this in all your interactions.

Perennial peace,
our daily practice.

Essence of the Soul

The essence of the soul comes into the world
to forget that it is a soul,
to once again remember that it is a special essence,
because it is fulfilling.
The more the soul forgets itself,
the more fulfilling when it discovers itself once again.
We are only empty long enough to be fulfilled once again.

Cold, hot, winter, summer,
up, down, sky, ground,

always changing and evolving.

The Battle

Much love to all who stay for the battle,
and also the times of rest away from the battle.
Love for the ever-lasting search of spirit thinking.
For the constant motion forward,
to strengthen the mind, body, and spirit in universal
understanding.
I don't know what kind of battle you have,
but I know the despair of mind,
can always be uplifted with the spirit within you.

Opening the Heart

Open the heart to the world,
then the love will overflow more abundantly to the people.

Universal Law

Keep your head up firm, with your truth and love.
And remember,
(eventually)
your good deeds.
They will always come to greet you.

For Your Heart

When you realize your life is a miracle, your benefit is in
realizing your success has already been achieved. Everything
accomplished by you is also a miraculous mystery.
Honoring your life in this way, and treating
all those around you like other gems, is the greatest
success. Let this settle within your heart.

Together

Who is teaching the children to hunt?

to cook,
to fight,
to love,
to heal,
to have fun,
to feel free,
to learn,
to be fearless...

to live,
to teach,
to understand,
to be strong,
to walk alone,

to walk together?

Love Medicine

The thought of everyone I've ever met
rushes through my veins.
Pouring energy of love through my eyes,
keeping my mind calm, still, and sane.

For we are all each other.

Intuitive Spirit

Kids are tuned in to spirit,
your energy is their real teacher, calm.

True Happiness

Learn to love yourselves as the angels love you.
Then you will feel a true happiness.

Divine Within

Be more loving than your father, your mother, your friends.
Look up to the universe creators, divine spirits,
great teachers of light.
Let them flow through you and guide you,
to beam out their presence
that is now so divinely within you.

Fairy Dust

Earthly Mother, you're the woman I feel divine love for.
I shower you always with love,
and hold you in my heart as my soul mate.

Every cell in my body is yessing you,
and the universe will keep blessing you.

This love is what every story teller wishes to tell,
sending love and fairy dust to all, like Tinkerbell.

Walking Faith

How we sit with our hearts and walk softly on this Earth,
shows how truly, spiritually faithful we are to the Earth,
and the wonders of love.

Self-Love and World Love

The more love for the self,
the more love for the world.

Dreams

If you have a dream,
no matter what anyone says,
if the dream is close in your heart
it can and will become a reality
if you want it to be.
It is inevitable!

What reality do you want to see?
Beauty and miracles all the time?
Or just a life of lost hopes?
It is up to you, my brothers and sisters!

Let this settle within you
with a calm,
but deep,
very deep,
vibrating drone sound,
like one of a Tibetan horn.
This frequency is for you.

From my higher wisdom.

Learning Love Is Our Daily Practice

Whatever helps you feel good and replenished,
whatever feels good to your higher purpose and highest good,
is for your body, mind, and soul.
Whatever it is you want to do in life,
remember you can do it.
Remember this is your life to live in a good way.
Stay around those who bring out the best in you.
Corrective criticism is always good,
harshness is never fun.
Love in a higher and healthier energetic way.
Be gentle with yourself and with others in your life.
Be firm
sensitive
open
aware
collective.

Learning love is our daily practice.

Remember

Remember to pray to the one,
feel the sun,
see all race in grace.
Remember to love the moon,
love the stars,
remember to love the planet that is ours.
Remember to love the creators, for they are the narrators.
Remember to love the teachers and all God's creatures.
Remember to love the universe,
and love yourself.
Remember, love your purpose,
and all on the surface.
Remember God is thy,
humble is why.
Remember to have faith,
be free,
fly with no worry,
and see the past fall,
for the spirit of God is in all.

The Light Comes Through

Angels are all around.

The more we know this,
the more we feel better and better,
seeing the miracles every day.

The light comes through us,
helping us to love each other,
as God loves us.

Star Teachers

Thank you for observing the moon
that sits before all the children on this Earth.
I will send you light and love in all my meditations.
The love you sent reaches me in sweet understanding
of unity and affection.
The stars listen to our every intention and gratefulness
that we send to them.
The love they send us is always there, ready to be felt,
and received
for those ready to comprehend.
This love is all around them and all around us.

The stars are our teachers.

In the Breath of a Moment

In a moment when you forget, or don't feel God's love,
look up to the sun and moon, the stars and the trees,
and know that they are watching down over you,
sending life force energy right to your feet, wishing you all the
best and waiting to once again connect with you.

Giving Thanks to God's Omnipresence
and Beauty

Thank you universe creation,
thank you universal mother and father,
your frequency is so very powerful.
Your essence and presence expresses much beauty of this creation.
Beauty that is of another place,
unimaginable to the human mind.

A Little Poem

Sit in meditation with your peers,
Send light for many years.
Listen to the truth within your ears,
Until you can smile in your mirrors,
Transforming your fears into tears,
And your love into cheers.
Follow the love in your heart,
Your heart will show you how,
Think wow take a bow
and sit in meditation right now.

Feeling Real Love Is Our Greatest Experience

Let love be taken in by all, with all it offers. No matter what
religions or spiritual practices we have as people, we must remember
that, in the search for love, we can realize that love
is at the base of all religions. So in truly looking for truth,
or being part of a certain spiritual group, or not,
we can realize God is always love.

This teaches us to always love our fellow human beings.

Love

Thank you for seeing the light in me that I see in you.
Your beautiful aura around you is one of pure light from the skies.
Truly I have not seen it often.
So when I look at the moon next time,
I will think that you are possibly looking up at the sun's
reflection also.
With the comfort of the universe's love
and thoughts of you after an hour meditation,
I will inhale nature's breath,
that we all share together.

Sweet day to you, reflection of light and love.

Soul Preparation

Someone said to me
that it is good to be grounded.
So I thought to myself
"Yes."
Once a person is grounded,
and pounded and pounded into the ground so much by this life,
that person cannot help
but want to be in the ethers of light in the skies.
Being grounded is getting our souls ready to fly.

Enjoying Life

Enjoy the sun and wind,
Love the love we are in.
Let your energy spin,
Remember life miracles happen now and then.

May all beings learn not to break,
But to bend.

In life there is no real end,
only the beginning,
of the beginning,
of the beginning.

I thank the angels for being in my life.

May we always remember them,
in all our interactions.

Love Is All There Is

Love from ourselves or others is what this world comprises
at the root of it.
How interesting, indeed.
Every day is a new day for us to move forward in a good,
loving way.

Words of the Heart

May your heart always speak a thousand words through one
moment and with one movement of your lips.

Patience, a Trait of God

Sometimes we want something so much,
and we can't have it.
This hurts us.
We know inside
if we do the work within,
we will eventually have whatever it is
that is for our highest good.
Because of our will to do the inner work,
and through that time lag of being at ease with patience,
it then feels like it comes to us
almost effortlessly.

Patience, a trait and a treat of God.

Hearing the Angels Whisper

I will wait for you 'til the end of time
For you to be able to join together with me.
And if you don't come home soon
I will still be waiting.

Our Angels.

They help our souls to become one with them in the flesh
To fuse with them joining them

So they can eventually take us home

To paradise.

My Meditation Altar

Sit pray,
know you will be okay.
Meditate contemplate,
feel your heart sing.
Divine human being,
start another day to make art.

Give be,
in love you see.
Be free to journey inward,
send light right to your friends and enemies.

Live strive,
you are alive.
Fit the flower in one hour.
The meditation,
to see the beauty of creation,
in every situation!

When you know your angels are with you,
they will gift you.

God's Flowering Essence

The flower brushed my face, reminding me of you,
a similar scent of your nature.
But nothing compares
to what can be truly experienced with you.

Our Freedom

Freedom is our greatest ally.
I love the Earth,
I love the sky,
I love big-hearted people!
I love letting my perception of this life
get full of love and light.
I love enjoying every day to the fullest.
I love being grateful for every moment.
I love learning about myself.
I love strengthening my soul.
I love my family
and my spirit family.
I love being here in this time,
on the planet with all of you.
I thank you.
I love you.
We will all get through this.

When Love Pours In

It's amazing how much love comes pouring into your life
sometimes!

Friends love all around,
lovers love enough to ground,
beautiful rivers of this joy at bay,
the essence of God is here to stay.

Our energy flowing freely uniting,
our light shines as bright as lightning,
connecting our awareness back to love,
is like holding our truth with a comfy glove.

Energy exchanging, the planets rearranging,
our minds start to align,
we wonder in love and patiently state
we are ready for our minds to be in meditation, to contemplate.

The love and light from the oceans below,
to the love and light from the skies above
reach us gratefully
Reflecting our bright connection,
to life and all things.

This Is Our Home

As divine souls on this Earth, humanity will always come up with new and improved concepts of God and we will individually live our own religious/spiritual lives. The key component is our growing awareness of ethical and moral values; love, compassion, empathy, understanding, and support for our fellow brothers and sisters on this planet we call Earth. This understanding can help humanity to live, share, and experience a more meaningful, happier, and more centered life. With prayers of light, our own daily worship, and meditations, we can clearly see the fruits of this creation. Living and educating ourselves in this realization, daily, is one of the best ways to awaken to our true, spiritual, and highest destiny.

Love Is My Religion

Let love be taken in by all, with all it offers.
No matter what religions people have they must all remember
that in the experience and individual search for God,
love is always the true religion.

Love your fellow human beings.

Love Comes In

Love comes in many different forms.
We can observe the uniqueness of all of them.
In the end, it is all love.

The observation of love is made possible
through the heart, mind, and body.
The spirit molecule within our brain,
and the light angels within us
and all around us
make it possible to have this realization.

So we are truly blessed!

I want to see love overcome all things in mind and body.
I want to see the spirit fill the mind and body
with joy,
truth,
and beauty.
I want to see this raise our frequencies,
so that one day
the whole planet is living life
in full gratitude and love for all life vibration.

Eternity

Wherever we go,
wherever we are,
we are all walking toward the same end/beginning,
as divine souls on this Earth.

This is very special!
Indeed.

Everything Everywhere

Every time I see people sitting still or moving around,
it reminds me to sit and move into meditation,
to drop into my own heart so I can be closer to the divine.

The Planet Teachers

The moon reflects the sun's light,
in the day and in the night.
We observe its glow in deep affection.
Our observation brings us to a realization
of a feeling of life's surreality.
We look at the moon
just sitting there in time and space
and we see our Earth
just sitting in space
as we calmly observe
being unharmed,
loved,
warm,
and able to breathe.

Ahhh . . . that's pretty amazing.
That is us having a religious experience!

For having love for life and for creation
is religion!

Knowing

I know that the love I have for myself, the world,
and the people,
is the most special thing ever.
No one can take this away from my heart.
This love will be with me for eternity.
This love is what the creators gave to us.
What a gift!

Perspective

There are many paths we could follow,
there are many options we can take,
there are many things that can happen,
remember we have great lives to make.

Seeing Eternity

Once you get to a certain level within yourself, you become a
leader and you enjoy being around others
who share a similar healing and giving frequency.
You don't remember how you got there, or why,
but it just happens through many years of practice.
The lights just turn on inside you
and you sit in awe,
remembering when you first aspired to be that.

You are what you want to see in others,
for that is a true and real reflection of yourself.

Thank you, Creator, for your ability to dwell within me, to uplift
my consciousness to join more with you,
in spirit unification and spirit fusion with the angels.

*To all beings in all the universes created
by our universal mother and father.*

For All Beings

When we fully tap into our hearts and we practice this daily,
the ones around us feel it, if they or we know it or not.

We can sense this love more when we are in a frequency
to feel this love within our own hearts.

It is then only a matter of time before we realize the true self,
the self that is connected to the higher self.

The self that chooses to be in more love and light
with and for all beings.

Gentle with Yourselves Always

When we remember who we are,
we realize that we are all divine loving beings in the universe
who came here to know, share, see, and be love,
gratefully humbled and happily realizing and
enjoying who we have now become.

Universe Creator

Just like you who are reading this,
and to all of us here on the healing journey,
we are always changing and evolving for the better.

I thank you so much for being a part of my life, universal creator,
in this time.
You have helped me so much to look more within
and to never feel without you.

Water of Beauty

Sweet tear-shaped feeling of love, gather to the surface of my heart
to observe these words of divinity within you,
to set this tone.
Like Dr. Emoto's study of the water molecules that change
with the frequencies of our thoughts and voices onto this creation,
transforming them into beautiful snowflake-like shapes,
like the sounds of thousands of beautiful recordings of our voices
being taped.

We step aside to watch what we put out into our universe,
observing these molecules,
hoping we make a clear and elegant mark one day
to show that we are honored and grateful to be here
with our paradise mother and father
in this amazing creation.

Meditate

Meditate

A Spiritual Age on the Planet

Light bright,
golden in the night.
Right sight,
Lift it light.
Shift uplift,
Give a gift.
Bring sing,
Give a ring
of light in the night
to help shine your brothers and sisters home.

Roam dome,
Coming home.
Earth worth,
Giving birth.
Information, sensation, creation, manifestation,
intuition, mission, nutrition.

Rebirth,
Evolve into love,
For the spiritual age is here on the planet and is coming now!

Nature Sounds

We sit, walk, and meditate in nature. In the grass, near the trees, we hear the birds singing in sync with the sound of the wind and leaves. We, too, look and seek the Divine in all things, hearing the love in the forests spreading angel wings. With nature sounds, birds, the smell of dirt on the ground, we find peace; here is where we share time, in this moment, connecting with the universe, angels, fairies, and ancient light beings.

Expressions of Love and Beauty

Amazing to be grazing on this,
an uplift,
a gift to those who sift, shift, and lift up their friends with their
creative nature, in cosmic unity, art, passion, fashion,
to create consciousness,
eternal bliss,
in the minds of those who never miss
a kiss,
from the winds that breathe,
weaving leaves,
trees,
bringing men to their knees, saying,
Please give us more.
For your show brings open doors,
happy inspiration to its floor,
taking people to their core,
in their values for love, not war!

A Simple Poem: The Love for Our Earth, Sun, and Moon

Eclipse, you are born again; you come from the sun's soul.
Your shadow first touches, then kisses, the tip top of our moon.
Our father sun's light shines from the back of the earth and to our
moon on this calm eclipse night where you are created and born.

The universe is letting us know once again
that the sun's light always shines on our Earthly Mother's back.
The sun's light shines onto the back of the Earth, reminding us all
that even the dark shadow of the moon
comes from the bright unconditional light of the warm and
loving sun.
Always bursting its light to all to show its everlasting and eternal
love for thee, Earthly Mother.

Birthing us into this new beautiful wave, closer to infinity,
where no one can limit me,
nor you.
Can you see this? These waves of love,
pouring daily through our infinite space,
to our heavenly, earthly place,
to reflect and protect
the potential life that our souls hold?

Our hands patiently wait to touch the sun once again.
Heavenly Earth, spin and spin
through the space of the universal mother and father.

Twirl and twirl,
for the pearl that you truly are.
Earthly Mother, can you see your own beauty?
All the stars fall onto you

wishing you a peaceful journey in the galaxies of galaxies. Let your
inhabitant children send you light.
Let these inhabitant children wish the best for you.

For without you,
they would not be!

The Light within Us

Activation for the nation.
Love, full of sensation.
Bliss that will never miss,
A love and a gentle kiss.

Give to live,
Love to give,
Seek to be,
Feeling free.

In light we unite and together we see

Love that can be
so fulfilling in this eternity.

Earthly Mother

Earthly Mother, don't cry,

for your heavenly skies are too beautiful and too sharing to be sad.

The universe loves you and the angels are with you.

Your glowing face expresses a true, pure, and loving heart,

worth a thousand heartbreaks to get to.

I am truly honored to have your heart, my loving mother.

May your heart always be full of love with angelic light and

vibrancy.

Because that is what I see you sharing with the world.

So you should inherently receive the same.

Love and Light

Face, face, face, face,
Face all things with no fear.
Live your life, your turn to steer.
Keep on flowing, keep on knowing
For your life is right here.

Wish it up, speak it out.
Love your own, hold it out.
Give your best, wish your love.
Kiss a face and spread your love.

Face, face, face, face,
Face all things within your mind.
Keep your love within divine.
Keep in mind your soul will steer,
Remember your angels are always near.

Face, face, face, face,
Face all people with some joy.
Face the world like a toy,
Play and dance and have some fun,
Send some love to the sun.

Face, face, face, face,
Face yourself with all this love;
Shift your hands with these gloves.
These nice gloves of words will keep you strong,
Sit in meditation all night long.

Happy Birth Day

I will begin my gratitude for life with this.
May we always treat every day as if it were our own birthday.
And may we always treat others
as if it were theirs.

Honoring the Women on Mother's Day or Any Day

Happy Mother's Day to all the women who have children,
and to all the women who don't.
You give so much love and life to the Earth,
even if you don't realize it.
So much nurture comes naturally from your being.
Your care and love is so important
to the survival of our species.
Thank you to all who honor this.
This love we share with you
truly expands the world
and universe
in more love and light.

Natural Giving on Easter or on Any Day

Give today to your friends,
family,
the ones you love.
With a smile or a gift,
or with a meditation sent with light.
Not because it's Easter,
but because we are human,
and that's just what we do naturally.

The Deities Are for All

We are here to learn lessons.
We all sleep under the stars in the sky. We shall never fall
but come to realize, and rise again!

To Jesus, Buddha, Krishna, Qwan Yin,
the fairies, the paradise parents, the angels and the universe.
The names don't really matter.
To myself and to you.

A Yogi's Heart and the Guru Within

I sit with the love for all beings born from a woman like you.

I am also a stargazing scientist of my own self in search of God. My will brings states of fate to my bleeding heart, into the unknown, covered in mere simplicity. The shadow of my unseen heart burns for the knowing and rest, to be at peace with where the world's direction is going. I sit sipping tea with God in meditation, hearing the loud sound of God through silence, breaking free from the torn minds of men before me.

Remembering, the rivers keep flowing, the sun keeps showing and the rains keep snowing, our hearts keep going and the universe is always showing that the Spirit is all-knowing. I know that I am you, you are me, we are one, so let it be.

The Guru Within will feel without if his fellow men and women, brothers and sisters, fall slow and are waiting in delusion's net. The Guru Within's secret wish is to wake up the few still not yet awake.

Our life is our movie!

So on set one, take two, take three to heaven's gate. With moments so few, I wonder who you are? For us, for me, for them, for us, it's a must to trust.

I am, you are, connected with galactic stars way out far. I give for free knowing I am you and you are me. So you see, in this we are always free.

We are ceaselessly unfolding! Do not worry; our team of light soldiers will rise up without sleep, gushing their hearts in solitude, deep within the divine. I find we are the rainbow children whom all the prophecies have shared about. One day no one will be without, breaking bread with roofs over everyone's heads. This should be the law and as you see there is a flaw. In meditation our souls give no breaks, laying the snake to rest. Our intuitive hearts say no deal, our lives are real. In meditation, truth enters the ears quietly, like music echoing through a tunnel. Our minds, still.

The universe shines its light into the deepest dark night of our world for all of you. Saying, "Remember what your brother shared with you: to have no worries, like the birds in the sky. You warriors are true. The spirit of Truth is lighting up the world with no one left behind. Our meditative heart fully shines, Love is always on my mind, it is all I strive to find."

God's love is divine; it's our time to shine.

The Warrior Soul Joining Together with the Spirit Mind: A Metaphor

I sit, mind clear, my breath remembers past wars,
battles of thousands of men in armor.
I feel as strong as the energy of thousands of men in armor,
I feel as strong as the thousands of warriors I have defeated.
My feelings for them are empathy and compassion.

I realize the strength it took
to stay brave in the darkness that incinerates mortals.
I have taken this time that I have been given to be in peace; to rest.
I never thought the time would ever come,
to experience this,
like this,
taking the time to prepare for light,
bright enough to blind anyone.
I walk forward trusting the memories
of the feelings of flying.
Still I sit in peace,
strengthening,
for what?
I trust, so why strengthen?
I sit, I act,
and move calmly, gathering information,
social status,
building up economic reality,
climbing, never wanting to look down,
but do,
to stay present in the reality of what was,
to see the creation and manifestation of what is now.
I am very thirsty.

The Love Poems

Reminder

To taste of your nectar would be so sensational,
I only wish to admire your beauty
and caress your loving heart with my own.
To give you some pure love
for you to always be able to taste it with just a thought.
To remember together,
that we are all one,
once again.

For Love I Bow

I bow for love,
and I bow
to kiss love's feet,
the feet of our Universal Mother and Father.

Life is My Greatest Relationship

Let all emotions flow like streams.
It's true love I feel in my dreams.

Cradled by my heart and its open doors, my destiny unfolds
to the sun and beautiful seashores.

With the ashes of my love, my lips keep falling to my own
two feet and Mother Earth's heartbeat.

This fertile soil in my chest expands and drips
love into my hands.

My heart melts, my body keeps lifting. The angelic source of
love and the force of God's power is behind me, pushing me into
greatness. My own tsunami of love supports my direction to blast
fast into the intuitive classes, into the temple, the gateways to the
great light and the heavenly doors, to share more love with
the Earth, my own heart, and all of you.

Gifts of Life

Where there is love, there is life.
Where there is a gift, there is a smile.
Where there is compassion,
there is an open heart for your beloved.

To Love

You light up my soul with cellular activation,
we vibrate a frequency that gives hope to all the world's people.
Divine love, Divine Earth, Divine life, you are a part
of my Divine soul.
I give thanks to the creator every day for you in my life.
We are one with the trees, the Earth, the animals, the plants,
the people, the stars,
the angels, the angelic orders, the fairies, the universe,
all the Earth helpers, and all the beings of pure light.
I love you, my love.

Soul Mate

My eyes cry today, pouring tears, for all the people who have
cried. My face wet, and then dried, wet, then dried.
My heart fills full with experience, and knows this pain
Like it knows the stars and rain.

I see my beautiful Divine soul, close to one with the same
Divine light. Pouring like a river, my heart is the giver,
It knows this pain.

In love,
A quick taste of what could be,
I know this love is always with me though, you see.

Giving tears for so many years of sight,
In my mind's eye,
I remember you that night,
In my temple filled with light.

Under the pyramid,
We shared years of our eternal love for each other,
In one moment,
That seemed like forever.

The taste of this love will forever be with me,
So sweet this love was, I will never forget.

I will sit with God in meditation,
And when these tears come again,
I will remember that this love will see me again.

And when that day comes,
We will be together,
And we will laugh in joy and say,
Remember when...

I love you, Divine love.
I am always with you,
Just like the angels are with you.
My love is pure, o so pure.

Love Is Falling from the Sky

Life is not about trying to fall in love with someone.
It's about falling in love with ourselves, so we can show our true
essence to the ones that we already love.

Divine Love

I felt the call of her eyes reaching for my soul.
What is understood is love so immense for those who come for a
gentle experience or a lift of spirit. I knelt down while she
touched my feet to kiss them,
I lifted her head high and said,

May you always find peace within the very path you walk.
May your own feet nurture you to be right where you need to be
on your journey. You are not for my pleasure or pain.
You are God's lovely child and you belong surrounded by
beautiful, colorful
light and joy. Let me wash your feet now, for your good nature
instills more love in the hearts of many; let your heart relax
while I embrace you as a sister, to nurture your hands that have
washed many pains from people's troubled hearts. If you truly
wish to be my divine love, dear one,
then it will be and I will rise to embrace you.

Divine Blue Skies

Divine blue skies and blue eyes gazing at the pits of my soul,
Sprouting love in meditation I always feel whole.

We watch the flowering of our love flowing in so deeply,
Flowing in so neatly,
I seek love completely.

Reaching love's surface,
I see the love blossoming, observing its purpose,

We sit breathing in the love for all beings,
Spreading it unto the hearts of so many out there,

We observe the universes,
Planets, stars, suns,
Blasting love to our chair,

With so much intention, love, and care.
When I look at those beautiful blue skies and blue eyes,
Love is the only thing I wish to share,

Comforting my soul in one moment,
Both our hearts beat,
And our eyes stare.

Our divine love grows so abundantly,
This love seems so unconditional,
So very rare.

I see the depth of angelic vibrancy, eternal divinity, infinity,
pouring out from within you,
merging with the deep divine love for the spirit of truth,
our universe,

That is also within me.

Eternal Light

Smooth walking,
Making tea,
Life of laughter,
O so free,

Giving thanks,
Blissful love,
Snuggles and cuddles with lots of hugs,

Prayer devotion is our magical potion,
Love and kindness,
Keeps our hearts wide open,

Awareness and beauty is our token,
Words of wisdom,
With no thoughts being spoken,

We glide through the day always blissful first,
After our meditations,
We wear our hearts on our shirts,

Sending love, giving light,
Bright as stars, shining in the night,

Knowing our hearts are more alive,
When the divine soul mate,
Has just arrived,

In Lakesh, I am inspired to be,
I am you,
and you are another me.

Bright lights flash together as we dash into infinity,
At the speed of light,
Where no one can limit thee,

O divine Goddess,
Sprinkle that star dust we make with our love,
Give it to those,
So they can fly like a dove,

Universe we give it all to you,
Because this love,
We know so true,

And it takes two to tango,
When our skies are blue.

Springs of Joy

Springs of joy spring forth from our tingling fingertips,
We emerge,
Our dancing energy clips,
Together they twirl and do flips,
Touching tips, moving hips, kissing lips.

Hours pass,
a walk on the grass.

Morning star,
I see who you are.

The love song melody dips,
Moisture falls and my heart drips,
I say I love you.
Oops, it slips.

Tears that once dripped,
Have now been sipped and wiped up by your lips.

Spiraling galaxies forming,
Temple lotus form swarming,
Our cosmic intuitive nature norm is coming back
To remember our hearts were past-life torn,
From the days we were born.
We have searched all over the Earth for this storm,
Together our bodies so warm.

Wet sweat breaks showing the love it takes,
And what passion it makes.
Tantra becomes our mantra and meditation our situation.
We listen to our hearts beat,
Baboom, baboom, baboom,
Again we enter the womb.
We know our angels are in the room,
Our lovemaking turns doom and gloom into angelic perfume.
Ring, ring,
I hear pleasure sing.

We are the Earth, the wind, the stars, and the rain.
The clouds sang. Love spun and Earth had begun.

Individually our bodies are mini-earths,
We as individuals are like our own cosmic universes,
We are all creations,
And we are all a part of everything we can see.

The consciousness doorbell rang.

Divine Beloved

Any moon coming from your sky body
is like starry chocolate milk for my body's sun.
I will sip your moon and caress your sky body,
filling my soul's thirst with a thousand suns.
We are parts of two solar systems coming together.
So of course our energy might spin a little 'til our planets settle,
aligning in their perfect time. I am the Earth. Welcome home!
Thank you for welcoming me, also!

Love Uniting

Devoted Love is for those who have wide open hearts.
Loyalty to Spirit is for those
who have truly kept their hearts open to a Divine relationship.

Angelic Love

Angelic love washes over me to relax my being,
to let the waters of God's essence be the moving force
that keeps me calm, quenched, and refreshed
in my thirst to have more abundant faith
in the universe and angels that pour out from the heavens
to assist all mankind and all womankind.

May we always let the beneficial waters of meditation
help our sight,
to see clearly within the peace, the reflection, and love
that washes over us in our meditations.

To cleanse our hearts,
so we can truly see beauty in all things and all beings.

Merkaba Galactivation

Love shoots out from my soul
when I am in love and already feel whole.

The rainbows shower down from everywhere,
this day is very rare.

Sacred love is appearing again,
sacred offering from the universe reminding me
to spin from within,

like the Earth spins in the sun and with the wind,
rising Merkaba frequencies make our water and Earth poles bend,

sending a wave of galactic information right to our core,
only helpers of Earth and the angels will live here on Earth
and others no more.

We are the rainbow children,
the children of light,

guiding others home,
in the darkness of night.

Sun rises up over the mountain,
we drink of the sacred fountain,

gazing at the blazing sun,
all hearts on the planet becoming one!

Heavenly Play

No work,
When I have your hand.

Only play,
When you walk with me to be alive,
a student and a teacher of life.

Graceful companion of the love of God.

Only love,
Only breath,
Only gratitude,
to be by your side while we represent the tools to stay clear and
humble with our fellow brothers and sisters.

I am yours.
I am yours to take with you.

Your class is my temple.

Open Doors in the Universe

The universe is always giving us what we need,
we have to have our hearts and eyes wide open to see it.
Awareness open, intuition open, heart open, discernment open.

My Divine Lady

Earth spins while living in perfect harmony in space.
Galaxies swing like a wing of the angelic orders of light.

So dark in the night these creations twirl like pearls, spreading
beauty for all to see.
So heavenly eyes engage the spiritual age
coming true for us to be.
Flowering lotus, our hearts always new.
Miracles, miracles, miracles, the flower of life, intrigues every
child, son, daughter, husband, and wife, giving us this day our
daily heavenly bed.
We are so grateful by those who sped up the creation and evolution
a long time ago.
We sit up watching in meditation as we are
spiritually induced and fed.
Led by the spirit our hearts channel, though our bodies of a
mammal.

We are the souls of God.
We bow our heads and nod. We give our hearts to God.

Once again, I wrote this for you. Divine love, I bow with you.

To Love I Bow

Bow to love,
show your respect,
the angels are watching.

Love in the Setting Sun

There in the wind a calm message from Earth,
the wind, the birds, the people;
hear them speak throughout all feathers, all nations,
all people, all tribes.
The essence of the Earth elements are flying high,
the winds are carrying the birds gracefully.
They drift, watching the setting sun;
they, too, see and know God's beauty.

Surviving Love

Love will always be fruitful when it is acknowledged,
with the motivation and remembrance of the magical spark
of beauty and goodness
that the universe gives us to remember to give to each other.
The universal spirit never fails to lead us to love.

Short Stories

I did my first vipassana meditation at home—seven to ten hours of meditation per day for one whole month. I wrote this on the first day.

Reincarnated to Remember Birth, Death, and Eternity

If you could remember your first days of birth, you would remember you came into this world of unusual frequency. You probably felt cold, wet, and naked. Your first instinct was to hold someone or to be held. Your muscles were so new they were probably able to move only a little bit to hold on to the person who seemed to have everything you needed: love.

As you grew older, but still a baby, you enjoyed all the love and nurturing you were receiving. One day you realized that the one thing that was most important to you in the whole world was your mother's and/or your father's love.

You loved the way your mother laughed and smiled. You looked at her teeth and were drawn to the sparkle and shine of the light reflecting off them. You enjoyed the experience every time she looked at you and put her hand on your cheek or somewhere else on your face.

One day you realized that you loved your mother so much that you always wanted her to be around you. In this moment you looked at her as a God. Eventually you realized that we all physically die, and your heart was sad and broken.

This triggered something in you. You realized how much you loved your mother and needed her. In this moment you realized how much you appreciated her and maybe even worshiped her. These were your earliest days and your first form of worship: your gratitude and love for this universal creation.

You would remember that you thought of all the ways possible that you could save her from death, and you tried to imagine all the ways everyone could live forever once they had passed into the next world. After that realization, you told her you loved her and that everything would be okay.

For me, a day had come when I fully realized, for the first time, that I was loved and nurtured by the universe. In my realization I fully knew that the universe lives on forever and so do we. In that moment my heart felt a huge relief mixed with sadness and joy.

On this day something got triggered in me. I felt so much love for being alive, and I experienced the universe as being very loving and nurturing. In that moment I realized how much I loved, needed, and appreciated the universe. It held me and loved me, and I held it and loved it. In that moment I realized that I also had much love for myself, my family, and all beings. My heart filled with a huge desire to show my appreciation and my gratitude, and that is why I love to meditate. Meditation is how I show my appreciation. I love to show my love by remembering the universe is love; it is that simple.

The Earth is our mother.

The love that the Earth and the universe gives us all should be everything to us.

This is how I feel about worship through meditation and how I feel about God's love for all people.

I wrote this on the second day of my vipassana meditation.

Awakened to Divine Sleeplessness

This is a story inspired by my spiritual thirst for truth, beauty, goodness, and the love that is God.

So I sit, pondering my life and what's taking place here.

Ahh, I remember my family and the smell of the pine trees, the smell of smoke from the fireplace, the open smell of cedar, and the beautiful woman who saved my life.

So I sit, feeling empty, with nothing to hold on to, with no agenda. I left the comfort of everything I loved and everything I had, and so I sit, I sit, I sit. I breathe in deeply knowing that we are all always connected by the spirit of truth and that it is within each of us. This binds and bonds us to something that we sometimes have trouble comprehending. The special unity and mutual love we share with our families and the mutual connection to life are far more special than we know.

So I sit, knowing that we all love the ability to love, the ability to think, the ability to feel, touch, taste, and drink. We love the ability to hold, to run, and to feel bold by our ability to seek. We are experimenting with our own ideas about reality and what it has to offer and what we can offer it. We love the ability to be in the now, not even knowing how we got here. I believe we are unconsciously experimenting with what we think works in our lives and what we think works for our world as a whole, without even realizing it.

We are like computers and recorders picking up information, knowing we can and will use it again one day for the betterment of all mankind and all womankind. Many of us feel like we are tuning in to something, tuning in to ourselves, tuning in to the Earth. Many of us are sensing that we are hearing life and creation speak to us, hearing the sound of the wind, the ocean, the breeze, feeling the animals, the grass, and trees. We wonder at times if we really are feeling each other, or if we are really feeling God.

I sit, knowing that many of us here on the planet believe that we are here for a purpose: to know truth, to feel mutual love for ourselves, our families, our friends, the animals, and all beings. We have the ability to comprehend that there is no beginning and no end, there is just right now. We live in the now, always and forever.

We hear ourselves, our intuition, and the spirit of truth. We are here together, in unity with one another, to hear and heal ourselves and the Earth. We can hear the trees speak clearly into our ears; we can hear the animals speak what they want to say, and we can hear all children and all beings' voices cry out for the same common desire to live; this is how we all thrive.

Now we sit, feeling that our human minds are ready for our hearts to take lead and start planting seeds for our world. We are here to merge with this consciousness and use every moment of every second of every day to remember that this is why we are here, to work together for one common goal.

We are all here to learn wisdom and values that are taught by our true spirit, the Divine spirit. Education must always be humanity's main goal. We must make sure that every human being has the basic things that they need to enjoy their ability to love. This is our Divine destiny: knowing the everlasting love in the human-to-human, brother-to-brother, sister-to-sister, father-to-mother, father-to-son relationships, loving all family members, friends, animals, and all beings.

I sit, calm, in the beauty of my own healing frequencies. I realize our conscious energy is here to enjoy this thirst for divinity and to be realized by all living and non-living people and beings. So as I sit, I sit, I meditate, and then finally I lie down. Slowly I grow restful; I am falling asleep, wondering if I should get up and write all of this down on paper.

I think of our impact on nature, this paper from a tree that gave its life, willingly or unwillingly.

I surely must have drifted off, for now, suddenly, I am waking from my dreams. As I awaken I feel a wonder and a beauty that is indescribable. I lie in this temple, surrounded by golden pyramids. I hear the sound of quiet solitude. It is so divinely quiet, I would hear a drop of rain hit my feet. Here, as I lie in this bed, in this spectacular temple, feeling a spontaneous and spiritually powerful urge, with so much thirst for God, to seek the divine ceaselessly, to seek the master in every moment as I lie here now awake, I cannot help but wonder if my urge is masterfully and spiritually induced.

Now fully awake and still, I sit up with a craving and a hunger for the comfort of the Divine. Love has instantly swept away every thought from my brow. Never have I felt such a desire to meditate and show my worship through my meditation, to seek to connect with my spirit and my higher self. I sit in the quiet, calm, sublime, and secluded beauty of this Divine temple, smelling incense and cotton. The fragrance seems to be drifting in from nowhere. I am taking leave of these writings now to become fully immersed in and merged with this beauty. I will return to write the rest of this story of the higher self after three suns have fallen.

Three days have passed.

I remember that, while in this temple, I could meditate as many hours as I wished or as many hours as my body would allow. I remember I got up and sat on the meditation pillows that were puffed up, as if they were sitting neatly in eternity. It seems as if no one had ever seen this beautiful temple before, in its own perfect place, with its own beauty and destiny. I thought, *This place feels like it has only been visited by spirits of pure light. Light beings, angels, and fairies from the most high God. This feels like a yogi's paradise.*

I remember that I sat in meditation and words just came through me with no effort:

I am surrounded in truth, love, and light. I am guarded, divinely guided, directed, selected, and protected. Anything that is not in my best and highest good, I release. Anything that is in my best and highest good I ask to come and stay with me and I send a blessing to the universe.

The words came out as if I had always known them. I thought, *I am here to sit with myself. I am here to sit with my higher self.*

I remember that, sitting up straight, I began my meditation, focusing on my breath, hearing the sound of quiet, knowing that the angels are always with me. This meditative state, which seemed like only moments, had lasted many hours. I took some deep breaths to bring oxygen into my lungs, my brain, my hands, my face, and my whole body, while feeling happy waiting for my higher wisdom to speak to me once again. I had experienced it many times before. With deep curiosity I asked my higher self a simple question: *What are you, exactly? What are we really doing here on Earth?*

The answer came: *I am a vessel of the spirit. I come from a paradise a long way from here. It is a long journey to come and be with you always, since you turned four years old in your journey in the flesh. One day you will die a mortal death. I will take you to the universal Mother and universal Father once you have fully joined me in spiritual fusion. We will fly through the vastness of space, through many different training worlds and mansion worlds filled with spectacular beauty; bigger worlds than you could ever imagine. One day you will even see a sea of glass. It is the landing site on a mansion world in the universe; it is a crystal 3,000 miles long and 200 miles wide.*

The landing site is used by the seraphim transporters and many other angelic beings that traverse through space. It's a meeting ground for many souls that are brought there by the transporters to reunite. God is destiny for all mortal children of light and life. This is your spiritual education. It is a standard of the divine, awakened mortal souls that are fusing with the all-knowing God, the divine spirit in the journey toward paradise. Most mortals will get to experience the fantastic, beautiful, incomprehensible wonders of God's unfathomable love and unfathomable worlds. You will truly remember these worlds throughout the whole of eternity, while moving toward your paradise parents.

I was astonished and slightly confused, trying to comprehend how all of this was possible. I sat humbly and asked, *So you are here to be my eternal guardian angel?* And you're *here to always love me? Wow! So in every way, you are my loving higher wisdom! And you are here to live within me throughout all my mortal life and I am here to connect with you? You are here to help me tap into you more, to tap into God more? So my higher wisdom is here to . . . ?*

I was so blown away at this idea that I forgot to breathe and had to pause. I knelt down to show my respect for this spectacular being sent from paradise, from the Paradise Mother and Father, creators of all life.

I heard the response: *Yes, I am your indwelling thought adjuster, your angel. I make it possible for your soul to survive mortal death. I am here to channel God.*

I bowed in humble service.

I wrote this on the third day of my vipassana meditation.

A Story of Our Guru Mind and Our Other Mind: Coming Together to Be One, in Simple Meditation

The Guru within Mind studies things that our Other Mind might not seek, making Guru's Mind meek and Other Mind a little weak. Guru Mind wants to help Other Mind to get strong and be able to join Guru Mind one day, in devotion to self-love and worship. One day Guru Mind said to Other Mind, "If you're not too busy on Facebook or worrying about stuff, would you want to come with me to God's temple? I would love to take you there." Other Mind said, "Okay . . . it sounds a little boring, but I will come."

So Guru Mind and Other Mind walked to the Guru's temple to visit God's throne. Together they sat there as Guru Mind was ceaselessly calm, still, and in a meditation zone. Guru Mind started calling in the Light and some guides to be by their side. Guru Mind and Other Mind were feeling so good. Guru Mind started feeling the heart and mind come fully alive again.

Devoted Guru Mind said to Universal Mother, Father, and Higher Self, "We know that you love us to come home to be with you every day. So we have arrived!" Guru Mind told Other Mind, "When I am at God's temple I always feel at home. When I am sitting in my meditation chair with my eyes closed, getting rid of all my mind's chatter and despair, I very deeply breathe in some fresh air as I sit here straight up, focusing on my breath and hearing the sound of quiet. When the mind is still and calm, Truth enters the ears clearly, like music echoing through a tunnel." Guru Mind said, "Always, after a little time in meditation, I can't help but think to myself, 'Ahhh, I am finally home again; I am finally here!'"

After a long while, they walked back to where Other Mind

lived. Other Mind said, "I like coming to your home, Guru Mind. Can we go visit God's temple again tomorrow?" Guru Mind said, "Yes, of course, Other Mind. You are always welcome."

So the next day they went to God's temple, which was Guru Mind's home. Other Mind said, "Guru Mind?" Guru Mind answered, "Yeeesss, Other Mind?" Other Mind said, "It feels so good to be here with you at your home and at God's temple. I would love to come meditate at God's temple again someday. This is not boring at all; I feel like I am at home, too. I guess, when you have a spiritual practice like meditation, it helps you feel better and I feel so much better now!" Guru Mind said to Other Mind, "Yes, it does feel good, doesn't it? At home with me, your Higher Self, and with God." Guru Mind continued, "I tell you what, Other Mind. You are always welcome to join me and to keep coming back to my home. God's temple is everyone's home, and you are always welcome." Other Mind said, "Okay, and will you always come with me?" Guru Mind said, "Yes. Any time you want to come, I will always come with you."

Here at my home, with my best friend Guru Mind, I sit writing this little story about meditation.

I love going to the temple with Guru Mind, and I love feeling calm, at home, and always able to breathe in lots of fresh air.

Meditation is something that feels really good, so I always love to share about it. I've learned from Guru Mind that meditation does so much for me physically, emotionally, and spiritually.

It even helps my friends, my family, the Earth, and the universe. At the temple I always feel at home.

You Other Minds out there, you are always welcome.

Your Guru Mind is patiently waiting to meditate with you.

A True Story of a Buddhist Master and My First Meditations

One sunny day I met a Buddhist Master from Thailand. I had been living near the beach in Encinitas, California, pondering whether to return to my original home. I felt that my life was running very thin, and that I might not have much time left to live. I was getting on a bus when I noticed a very kind-looking man sitting in one of the seats. I sat down a few rows in front of him and the bus started to move. My eyes were drawn to this person; he had nice glowing skin and a caring look in his sparkling eyes. Not wanting to stare, I looked out the window, enjoying the trees and the sights of the beautiful town of Encinitas.

The bus stopped. I took a deep breath and got off the bus. The door shut, and the bus drove away. I quickly realized I had gotten off too soon. But it was all in divine order. The unknown person who had caught my attention on the bus had also gotten off. He walked up to me. Taking my hands in his, he told me that he was my brother. With a big, loving smile and a caring look in his sparkling eyes, he told me that he had traveled here from Thailand. His words were like raindrops, with the pure essence of a meditative mind. I was very curious about this special, intriguing person. He asked me if I wanted to go to the Self Realization Fellowship with him.[*] I thought that sounded nice, so I said, "Sure." From that moment on, I knew it was going to be very a special day.

---

[*] Self Realization Fellowship (SRF) was started by Paramahansa Yogananda in 1920 to spread worldwide the teachings about Yoga, the science of meditation, and to spread consciousness in connection to all the great religions for the cause of unity.

Sensing the Spirit:
The 80-Year-Old Buddhist Virgin

We sat, conversing, before going to SRF. He told me he knew the Dalai Lama. He said that when he first met the Dalai Lama he was told by the Dalai Lama that he was not to bow to him. The Dalai Lama pulled the Buddhist up when he was bowing and the Dalai Lama started bowing to him.

We sat there enjoying the sunny day and started sharing stories. After he showed me some photos of his travels, I was very pleased to show him my native flute. I had been playing the native flute a lot at the time and I always had one with me. My new friend was so excited to blow his breath into the flute! I felt such a strong connection to him in just a short amount of time. I sensed that he was different from anyone else I had ever met. He acted differently; he had so much vibrancy for life and looked all around him, as if he were a child going to the fair for the first time. It was fantastic and fun being with him as he experienced life. I had never seen or felt anything like this with someone before. He glowed with light and had a high vibrancy of spirit. He was a man people would follow around if they could, drawn to his energy, as described in stories I'd read of Paramahansa Yogananda and the effect he had had on whoever was in his presence.

My conversation with this fascinating man had a big effect on me. He told me that he had been in Thailand most of his life. He became a Buddhist monk at 21 and devoted his life to clearing his karma. Before we went to SRF, he took me to meet a woman who had also devoted her life to being a Buddhist monk. While we were at her home, he suggested that we both make lunch for her. He explained that she was a very special and devoted Buddhist who had chosen to be celibate her whole life. An-80-year-old Buddhist virgin! We all sat together, talked together, and laughed together. I looked around and noticed pictures on her wall of Buddha, Jesus, and another Buddhist man. Later I found out from this devoted 80-year-old Buddhist virgin that she had a whole collection of books written by the very man who had brought me there. He was indeed who he said he was . . . a simple Buddhist monk.

The Glowing Buddhist in the Picture

We had a very nice, stimulating conversation about the monk's family in Thailand; he told stories about himself, from when he was younger. I remember that, later, my new friend sat quietly in the living room of the older woman's home. He was just sitting there, silent and calm, with his eyes closed. He asked me to come sit with him so we could both meditate together. I did not know how to meditate. I had read lots of books about yoga and the universe, but I really didn't feel comfortable just sitting there, wondering if I was doing it right or not. I was way too shy at the time to ask him if I was doing it okay. So I just sat there feeling a little unsure of what to do, peeking at him, wondering exactly what he was doing, while he sat there with his eyes closed in meditation. I saw him focus on his breath, sitting up straight, as he held both hands together over his heart.

After the meditation he suggested that we take a short nap. He said, "If you are tired, sleep. If you are hungry, eat. If you are thirsty, drink." I was tired, so I accepted the offer. Upon waking from a restful nap, I again noticed the three pictures on the woman's wall. I quietly asked our Buddhist hostess, "Who is that, the man with the short hair wearing the Buddhist robe, in that picture right beside the pictures of Jesus and Buddha?" She said, "That is the very nice man with whom you have become friends. He was one of the head Buddhist Masters of Thailand. That's a picture of him when he was younger, with short hair." And so I learned from her that this Buddhist man, who I was spending time with, was in fact a very, very, amazing man.

We wanted to get to SRF before it got dark, so we got our things together. We were about to leave the house when the woman said to my new friend, "Here, you can borrow this flute if you want to play it." His eyes widened in amazement. He eagerly took the instrument and started to play. He was so excited to blow into a flute again! Twice in one day! It didn't make a very good sound, but he was so happy. He thanked her, and we left her house.

The Day of Awakening

As we headed to SRF, which was near the beach, on what was turning out to be an extraordinary day, my wise friend whispered to me, saying, "I was a devoted Buddhist from a young age. For 36 years I meditated in the forests, in a little house near a creek. I only came out here and there to hear my master speak and to meditate with him." He smiled a big smile and with sparkling joy told me, "My master also meditated most of the time; he rarely came out to teach. When he went to the forest to meditate in nature, all the animals and reptiles would come to be near him." This vibrant, happy man again smiled a really big smile, and again with his sparkling joy he said, "My master told me that he would pass away on a certain day. A year later he died exactly on that day, as he had predicted he would. He died in his temple, sitting straight up in meditation pose."

My new friend said that one day his fellow Buddhists declared him a master. He told me that he traveled, taught, and spoke in front of thousands of people in and around Thailand for many years. The people came to hear him speak his poetry and speak of his love for them. He even spoke to people in front of the Thai government officials, but they became wary of him because of his large influence. Eventually, the government banished him from the country. His face, usually so full of joy, looked sad and concerned as he told me this part of the story. "So many people came to hear me speak my poetry and love that the government became scared and accused me of acting like the prime minister of Thailand. That confused me, but I realized that some governments are corrupt and greedy for money. Suddenly, after being the most loved man in Thailand, I had to flee from the country."

This great wise man traveled to the United States after being told that he would never be allowed back into Thailand, not even to see his family. He smiled at me with joy and said, "It is okay, for my mother and my family know that I love them very much. My mother helps people feel better with her herbs, and my father is a calm, nice man with a military career." We continued walking toward SRF. We walked by the beautiful garden near Swami's Beach in Encinitas. My friend took me to a place where we could meditate together again, at SRF near the garden, overlooking the ocean.* Together we quietly watched the beautiful and colorful sunset. These were my first meditations with a true and real Buddhist Master.

---

* My poem "The Zen Sets" was created in remembrance of this beautiful person and this incredible day.

The Devoted Buddhist

Meeting, spending time with, and hearing the stories of this inspiring man was one of the major catalysts that caused me to begin my own meditation practice. The Buddhist man taught me to set my intentions and to feel the love that I have for myself before I begin my meditation. Then, he said, I must feel the love I have for my family, then the love I have for my friends, then the love I have for all beings. He told me that this intention is very powerful and that it is both important and useful to do this. My master-friend enjoys being an undercover yogi these days; he does not want to draw attention to himself. He taught many people for many years, and now he chooses to be unknown. This is why I have not shared his name. When he still wore Buddhist robes, before he grew his hair, people followed him everywhere he went. I could see why they did; I longed to follow him myself. His very caring and nurturing energy causes people to want to be around him.

Very rarely do we meet a person who has devoted his whole life to meditation and to clearing all past, present, and future karma. Now there had been some changes in his life. He excitedly shared with me that he was going to school to learn how to write in English so he could translate the writings in his books from his own pen. I asked him where he stayed when he was in San Diego, and he smiled and told me that he sometimes slept on the beach at night. I asked him if he got cold, and he told me he buried himself with sand to stay warm and kept a little mouth hole in the sand to get air. But he also shared that he sometimes slept at a really nice lady friend's house. He told me that when he was there, he treated the woman's son as his own. I asked if he liked her, and he graciously smiled, giggled, and said he did. He told me that now he gets to experience all the pleasures of being in a relationship with a woman, but he cautioned me that intimacy should only occur once or twice a month, no more than that. That story made me happy. I thought that perhaps his long, devoted Buddhist monk practice had included celibacy. He said he sincerely wants to live and experience things like a normal person now, just to experience life without teaching. He said he might teach again someday, but not now.

Now he wanted to experience life.

This man is an extraordinary human being. This beautiful person loves his homeland. He has so much wisdom to share with the world. I was caught off guard when we parted that first day; I could not stop crying. As he left I asked him where he lived. He told me he lived in Oregon. He said he stays with doctors who love to study him. He explained that his whole life has been committed to being free from attachments; he turns down offers for houses, cars, and land. He has never taken anything.

An Amazing Woman and Her Divine Gift

Other inspirations led me to continue on my meditation journey. One of them came from a remarkable healing journey I experienced. I had had a series of car accidents and other injuries, and I was feeling my life energy wane. I felt like I could die at any time. I had met the marvelous Buddhist Master and that had kept me going a little longer as I began my meditation practice. I was fighting to stay alive. I told my friends and my co-workers in Encinitas and Solana Beach good-bye. I had tried everything from working, to moving back home with my parents, to living in the mountains with my sisters, nephews, and brother-in-law. I was trying to rest and recover from whatever was making my body shut down. I tried fasting and eating raw foods. I received energy work. But nothing was helping. My sweet oldest sister was unsure why I felt like I was dying; she thought I looked fine. But inside I was struggling.

Finally she heard my distress and took me to a gifted woman. This woman could tell me exactly what was wrong with me by tapping into my body and listening to what my innate wisdom wanted me to know. She was able to hear my body speak clearly in her ear! She repeated to me exactly what my body wanted to say. She also told me, "If you are open to hearing the truth of what the innate wisdom of the body says, it has a beautiful way to help you heal faster in the most unexpected ways. The body knows best, as it has its own networking, intelligent force, and it is able to work with all the other forces within your body."

Helen was really open with me. When I was ready for more information after the treatments, she shared with me things from her own life. She told me how she got where she is in her own understanding of healing. She spoke to me about her meditation practice, her job, and what she realizes about her life and the treatments she gives through listening to the innate wisdom of people's bodies. Some people who have gone to see her call her the Body Whisperer. I just call her Helen.

Helen also taught me more about the sublime benefits of meditation and how far a person can get when being tuned in and in touch with themselves. This woman, who coincidentally worked in the same office as my sister, literally saved my life. I am blown away by all that she was able to do; she truly changed my life. This was my second meeting with a real master.*

* I created the poem Reflection in remembrance of this beautiful person and this wondrous day of discovery at her office.

The Devoted Woman and Her Gift

To this day, I have not seen or heard of any person who can come close to doing what Helen does. I have never experienced anything so advanced from anyone before. After working with me for almost two hours of treatment, this amazing woman lovingly told me that if I had waited one more day to see her, I would not be here right now. She told me it was a miracle that I was still here and that I was still alive.

After the first treatment, one of the things she said to me was, "Wow, you were just barely holding on by a thread!"

I have experienced things with her that were so profound that I know for sure that most people might not believe me if I told them. I do know that the people who have gone to see her and have experienced their bodies speaking are people who I can share a simple knowing with. I know that there are angels for sure, and incomprehensible and beautiful things going on right here on Earth. I have heard things from my body, my wisdom, my heart, my strength, and my power, and I have heard the universe speak to me clearly during my treatments with Helen. There are so many unexplainable things that have happened that I must believe that life is a miracle. I remember going to my last treatment with Helen, my new best friend. I was leaving to go visit Oregon to consider moving there. Helen, once again, somehow knew everything she needed to know for my best and highest healing.

The Body and the Universe's Voice

Helen knew I was on my way to Oregon. I did not even tell her. The whole hour-and-a-half treatment was spent listening to my body speak its higher, innate wisdom. Most of the treatment was about my going to Oregon and my being ready to go. As I left the treatment, Helen said to me, "Hey, you're really going! I am so happy for you!"

I remember thinking, *How does she know exactly what is going on with me?* She knows me better than I know myself, but from all that I have experienced with her, I also thought, *Oh, yes, well . . . she is super in-touch.* I am not even surprised any more. If someone said to me that they had seen a fairy, an angel, or a ghost, I might not believe them if I had not seen it for myself. Yet I know now the realities that are true.

I am still blown away by my experiences of hearing my body speak through Helen. I think it is a little funny that my sister and I bragged to each other and laughed about what we had experienced in treatment with Helen. Jokingly, my sister said, "Oh, well, my higher wisdom said that I have a heart of gold." And joking, I said, "Oh, well, the universe said I am a very rare and open-hearted person."

I love that Helen is so devoted to simple meditation and so connected to the universe because I would not be here if she wasn't. I remember being sad because I was going to really miss her, and my family, too. I had experienced her treatments once a month for a whole year. Not only am I still alive, but I know that the treatments saved my life and cleared the way for me to be who I am today. I am truly honored and humbled to know Helen.

Intuitive Voice

No matter how strong the intuitive voice is,
if you are not opened and wanting to hear it,
you won't.

When you realize your gentle intuitive voice comes with an
important message, then hopefully you will learn to listen
attentively to what words it speaks.

Silent meditation:
One of the keys in learning to listen to your innate wisdom and
to rediscover how to more effectively express your own heart.

Divine Intention

The mind leads the heart to the desert.
The heart leads the mind to paradise.
Together they can create more paradise wherever they are.

Expressions of the Heart

We express ourselves
because something in our hearts wants to be fulfilled,

or maybe it is already fulfilled in some way.

Finding out which it is can take some time,

or even a lifetime.

Benefits of Meditation

When you first start to meditate you will notice a calm, relaxing feeling, but come two, three, four months later you will be amazed at how much better you feel energetically, and you will be able to naturally see even more beauty, truths, and love in all of life. Then positive things will begin to unfold in front of you like sweet loving gifts down the road. For when the mind is still and calm, truth enters the ears clearly, like music echoing through a tunnel.

Divine Love: Simple Tools for Meditation

If you are curious about what meditation can do for you, I encourage you to find some time, even if it is just five minutes, to sit down and meditate. A simple way to meditate is to sit on some comfortable pillows that will support you in sitting straight. Sit up, cross your legs or have your legs straight out, with your back straight. Set the intention to be with yourself and with your higher self. Say to yourself or out loud, "I am here to sit with myself. I am here to sit with my higher self," and sincerely mean it. Set a timer for anywhere from five minutes to an hour. Then, sitting in a quiet, dark room, focus on your breath. Focusing on the breath is the purest tool for meditation. You can use ear plugs and turn off the lights, too. Having it dark is not a must; it is just easier on the eyes that way.

You can go back and forth between focusing on your breath and listening to the sound of quiet. Keep your back posture straight; it aligns the chakras and helps the chi energy to flow. Remember that your thoughts will always be flowing through your mind because you do have a brain. The more you meditate, the easier it gets to relax your mind and body. Feel the love that you have in your heart for yourself, your family, and for all beings. Feel the love of the universe all around you. Know that what you are doing is working to tap in more deeply to your heart and universal mind. The meditation is working, even if you think it is not. This shows the universe and the angels your thirst and that you wish to connect with them, with yourself, and with your higher self. Meditation is simple, and it works. Work up to meditating an hour per day.

After you meditate, there is a simple, little, positive thing you can do to enhance your life. You can write down the positive things you want to see happen in your life and for this world. For example: "I want to get good grades in school. I want to see myself graduate. I want to see myself being surrounded by loving people all the time." Okay, you get the point. Pick out a special place and choose a special crystal or something sacred to you. Then take what you wrote down, along with your sacred object, and set them in your special place that is charged with your sacred energy. Leave them there, charging. Every day for one week, add another list of positive things that you write down. At the end of the week burn your writings and release the energy of your wishes to the universe. Between doing this and your meditating, great things will unfold in your life. I promise. This stuff really works. I have seen miracles happen. This gets your mind in practice to intend positive things you want to see happen in your life and start noticing the positive things you can create in our world.

When I meditate, after I say that I am here to sit with myself and I am here to sit with my higher self, a little thing I do is ask Buddha, Jesus, the fairies, Quan Yin, and all the spirits of pure light to come sit with me.

Sometimes, before I start, I just imagine there are loving angel family helpers hugging me and I send light and love to my friends and family. This helps good energies to flow out into the world and it helps manifest more beautiful and positive events to become a greater part of our reality. Imagine sending people and the world love and waves of light while you are comforted, and know the angels are with you.

The True Value Giver

Know that any longing or loneliness we have inside of ourselves are just the little reminders for us to be more aligned with ourselves and source, more aligned with the universe. The angels and all beings are here to support us.

The world is here to support us. Remember to look in your mirrors and tell yourself all the great things that you love about yourself, all the beautiful things that you want to accomplish for yourself. You have the power within you to be happy, fullfiled, vibrant, and healthy. I believe in you.

Keep spreading your love for this universe, my friends.
Real friends are of God's universal love.
What a gift!
It's good to hear the universe is being seen
as a blessing to you.
Love is all that is and is all that is of value.

The Golden Chain

I am a masterpiece, I chip away at the illusions of the world,
Filling my heart with light and love.
Flowing through the waters of love, I find the keys to the spirit
expansion. This mansion holds the golden chain.
Sat Nam, Wahe Guru!

I Live for Divine Awakening for a Living

Whatever we do for a living, or what we accomplish, if we are
practicing silent meditation, once a day, once a week, once
a month, or once a year, then we are truly helping ourselves
to love and heal ourselves so much more. Keep reaching
ceaselessly to manifest your full potential! Fully love
yourself and truly look inward and clear your pains
that may cause you suffering!

It is up to you to know who you are.
It is up to you to create peace within your mind.
It is up to you to stay positive.

It is up to you to look in a mirror and tell yourself all the
positive and loving things you want to hear, and that you love
you, and that you want the best for you. It is up to you to reach
for the stars and realize you are made from stardust. Made
from love. Made for life. Made for greatness. Made for giving.
Made for you. Made to be a good friend. Made for a good
partner. Made from God. Made to be as much in touch with
your higher self as you can be. There is no time to lose.
Only time for you to choose.
For this world is waiting for you to step up so it can give more
to you, which you are now realizing it is here to do.

This brings a spiritual reward.
Material rewards, I am sure, will undoubtedly follow.

Love to All People, for a Spiritual Age Is Near

Materialism will wilt the spirits of men and crowd the mind
with useless matter. Only those with the knowledge and thirst
for spirit will remain in an eternal body. We can enjoy our
normal needs being met with ease or hard work. But let those
who shadow our minds with false media in order to instill a
false happiness, learn to repent for leading their brothers
and sisters astray. Let the knowing of pure heart love
within your soul, and the spirit within you, teach you
to see the fruits of righteous living.
Let all human beings know grace and see love in every face.

May all beings live, always having their simple needs met.
May all beings accomplish the restoration of the balance of
wealth to all the people of the Earth and may every human
being hold this with high regard,
to restore this balance.

When the materialistic thinking falls away from the minds of
the people, then we will see a spiritual age on the planet.
Be in joy about this, for it has been way too long that the kings
and queens have walked over the people of the Earth.

Hear the angels' voices in the winds and rain, see them shine
down from the sun and stars, feel them right by your side,
be one with them,
they will guide.

Listen,
can you hear it?
There are good things to come.

You are the one,
who has been waiting for you.

Stay fulfilled in the divine reality and always
strive to give better love to yourself.

Always Count Your Blessings

Through the Universe and Back

When we search to the ends of the universe, to the seas of the underworld, to find peace within, one thing we find in that state of clarity is the experience of doing what feels good. Throughout our journeys we learn great lessons about what makes us feel good; we also see the consequences for doing what feels good without proper introspection of what serves us in the highest in our day-to-day lives. Sometimes we are swayed or distracted by only ourselves. From our openness, wisdom eventually flows into us to guide us home, to align into our bodies to do what feels good in our day-to-day lives, with the sweet knowing of what that truly is.

We Are the Chosen Ones

In this moment you chose to read this, and you, for some reason, were drawn to this book. We are the light warriors, the rainbow children, we are what the prophecies have talked about and we were born for this time on Earth. We are a special gift; we are part of this whole creation—a gigantic creation, with trillions of planets, beings, angels, and universes.

Our short earthly life is but a small journey to our new heavenly home after this one. We must remember who we are. We are most likely talked about in other places in the galaxies, about how brave we are to have come to this world. Listen to your heart and know the universe loves us all. We will realize this more and more as we all evolve closer to eternity.

Within You

Look within for your light.
Ask the angels and guides to be with you.
Tell them that you are humbled to work with them.

The next pages of your life are for you.

Your turn.

I hope you truly enjoyed!

To send a donation or to contact me, visit my website **theundercoveryogi.com**.

Or my Facebook page **facebook.com/theundercoveryogi**.

Greatly appreciated!

Help out in a big way and let people know that reading this book online will be so much nicer on our trees. Remember to stay in your hearts, meditate, and keep up the good work.

Thank you again, with lots of love.

19291926R00104

Made in the USA
San Bernardino, CA
21 February 2015